JOHN CORIGLIANO

ETUDE FANTASY

for Solo Piano

Ed. 3221

G. SCHIRMER, Inc.

DISTRIBUTED BY

HAL•LEONARD®
CORPORATION

7777 W. BLUEMOUND RD. P.O. BOX 13819 MILWAUKEE, WI 53213

NOTES

My ETUDE FANTASY is actually a set of five studies combined into the episodic form and character of a fantasy. The material in the studies is related most obviously by the interval of a second (and its inversion and expansion to sevenths and ninths) which is used both melodically and in the building of the work's harmonic structure.

The first etude is for the left hand alone—a bold, often ferocious statement which introduces both an opening six-note row (the first notes of the work) and a melodic germ (marked "icy" in the score) which follows the initial outburst. This etude reaches a climax in which both the row and the thematic germ are heard together, and ends as the right hand enters playing a slow chromatic descent which introduces the next etude—a study of legato playing.

In the short second etude both hands slowly float downward as a constant crossing of contrapuntal lines provides melodic interest. The sustaining of sound as well as the clarity of the crossing voices is important here.

The third etude, a study on a two-note figure, follows—a fleet development on the simple pattern of a fifth (fingers one and five) contracting to a third (fingers two and four). In this section there is much crossing of hands; during the process a melody emerges in the top voices. A buildup leads to a highly chromatic middle section (marked "slithery"), with sudden virtuosic outbursts, after which the melody returns to end the etude as it began.

The fourth etude is a study of ornaments. Trills, grace notes, tremolos, glissandos and roulades ornament the opening material (Etude I) and then develop the first four notes of the third etude into a frenetically charged scherzando where the four fingers of the left hand softly play a low cluster of notes (like a distant drum) as the thumb alternates with the right hand in rapid barbaric thrusts. This leads to a restatement of the opening 6-note row of the fantasy in a highly ornamented fashion.

After a sonorous climax comes the final etude, a study of melody. In it, the player is required to isolate the melodic line, projecting it through the filigree which surrounds it; here the atmosphere is desolate and non-climactic, and the material is based entirely on the melodic implications on the left hand etude, with slight references to the second (legato) study. The work ends quietly with the opening motto heard in retrograde accompanying a mournful two-note ostinato.

J. C.

Performing time: 18 minutes

The premiere, by pianist James Tocco, took place in the Kennedy Center, Washington, D.C. on October 9, 1976.

ETUDE FANTASY

Commissioned by James Tocco on a grant from the Edyth Bush Charitable Foundation, Inc., for the Bicentennial Piano Series of the Washington Performing Arts Society, and dedicated to the memory of Edyth Bush.

ETUDE FANTASY
for Solo Piano

Edited by James Tocco

John Corigliano (1976)

Etude Nº 1: For the Left Hand Alone

*) All small notes throughout piece are to be played at the dynamic level of the large notes (in this case **ff**)

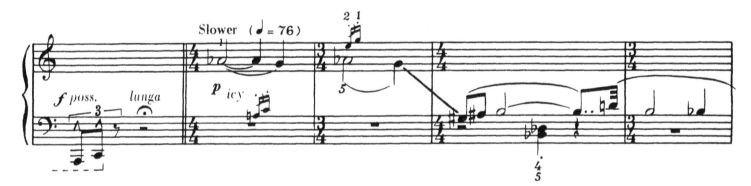

4

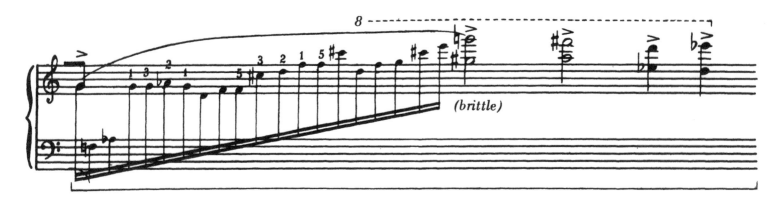

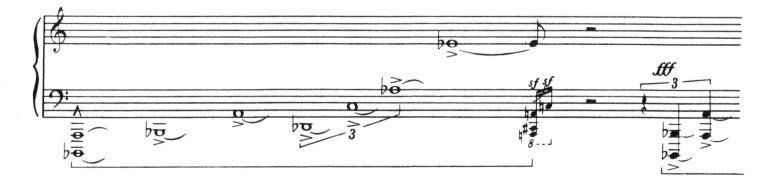

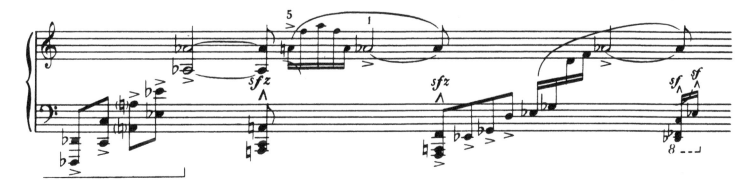

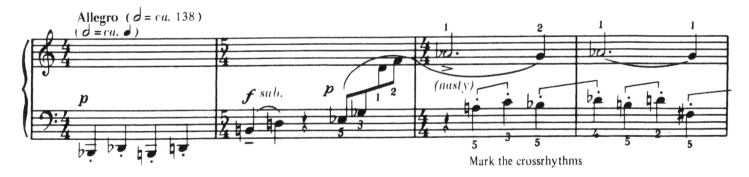

Mark the crossrhythms

6

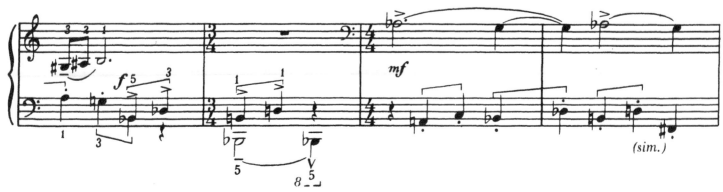

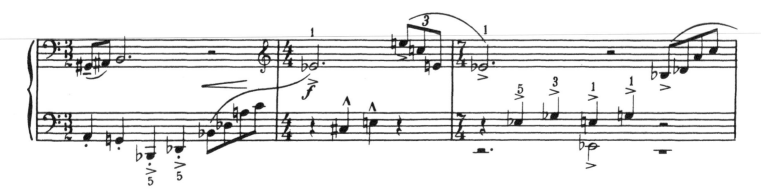

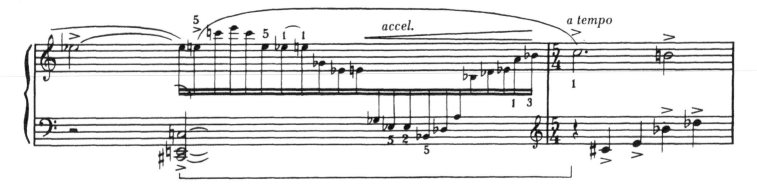

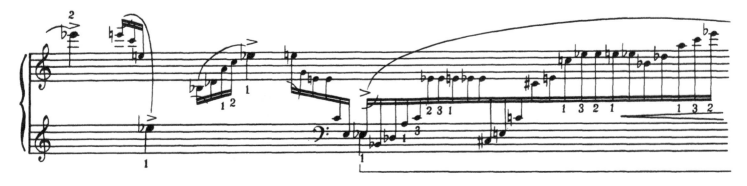

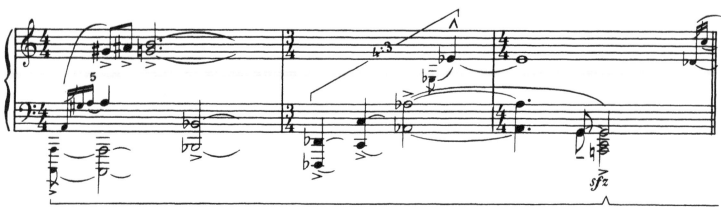

Allegro ♩ = 80

(con pedale)

♩ = 60

no accents

*) Imperceptibly change to legatissimo (Etude No. 2) and relax to ♩ = 60

Etude Nº 2: Legato

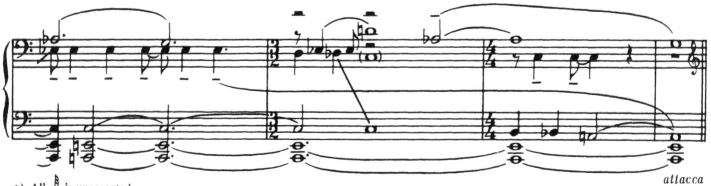

*) All ♪'s unaccented

attacca

Etude Nº 3: Fifths to Thirds

Allegro Scherzando ♩ = 100

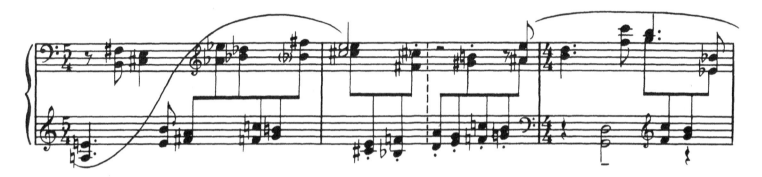

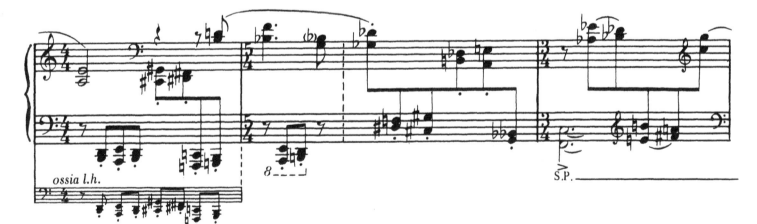

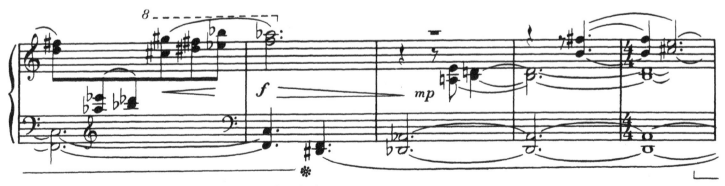

*) Play the phrased melody legato; other notes are detached

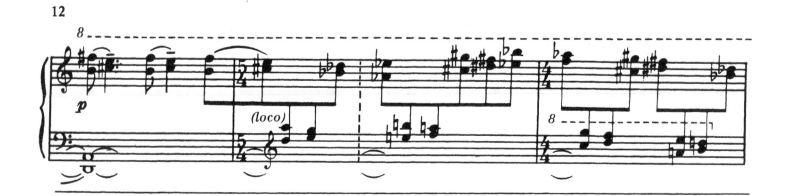

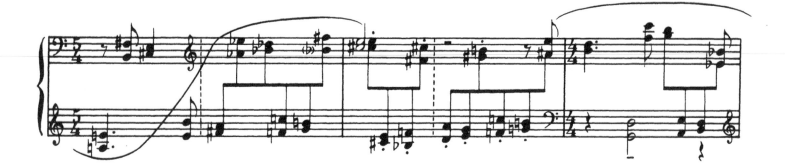

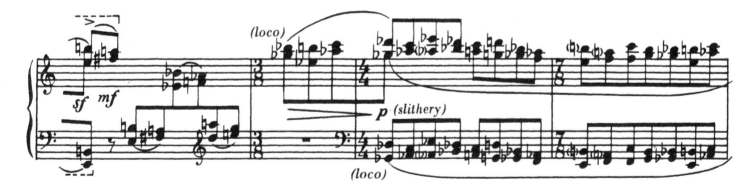

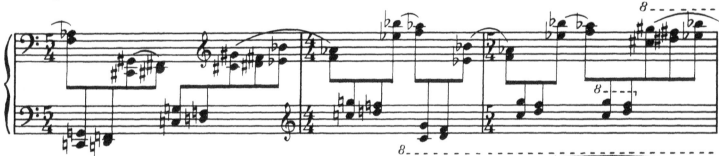

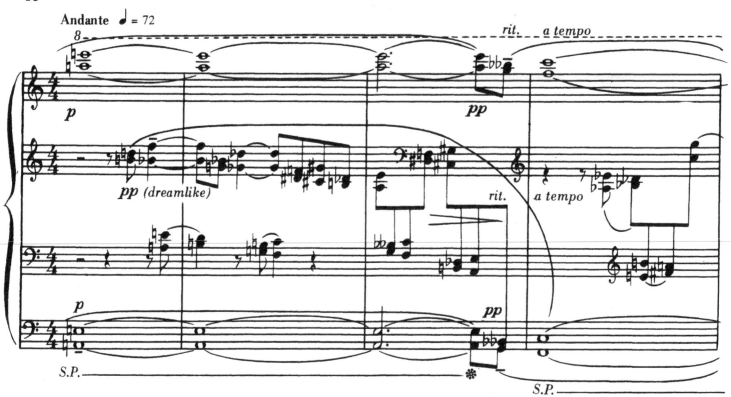

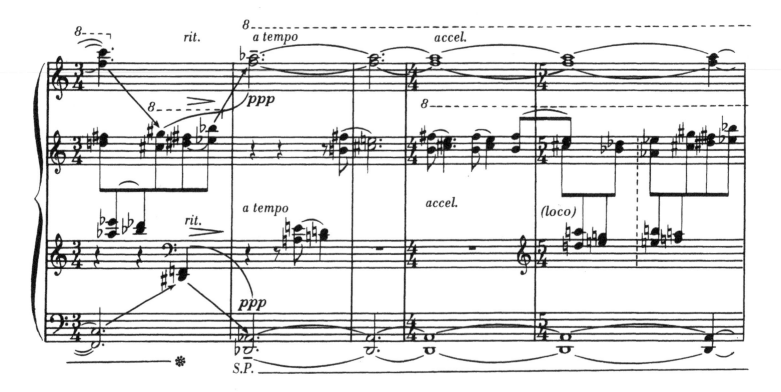

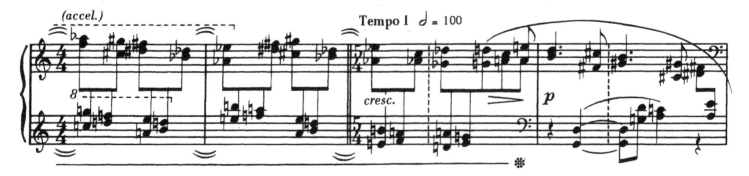

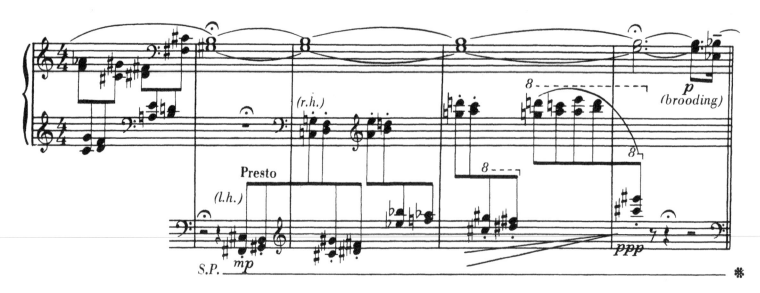

Etude № 4 : Ornaments

Andante ♩ = ca. 69 *(very free)*

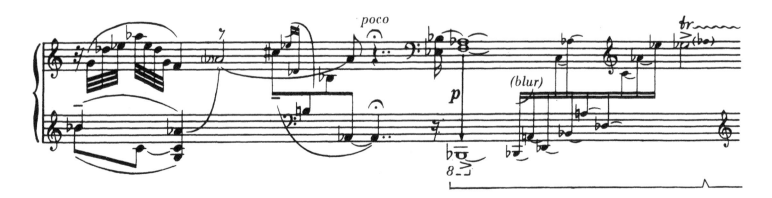

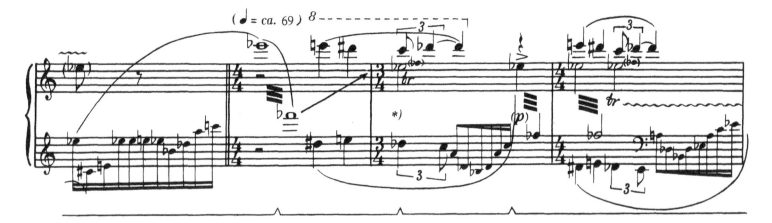

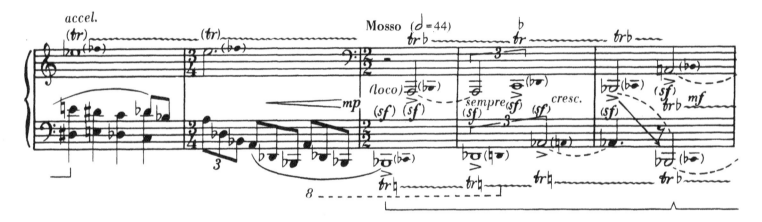

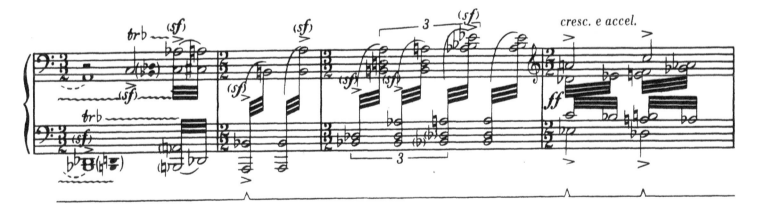

*) The change from tremolo to trill must be inaudible

**) Clusters to be played with the heel of the hand on white keys

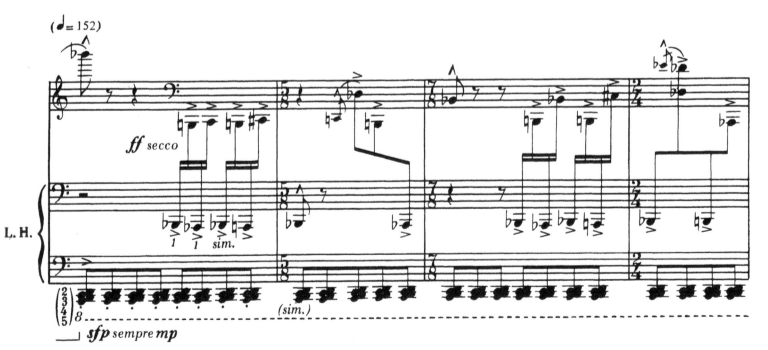

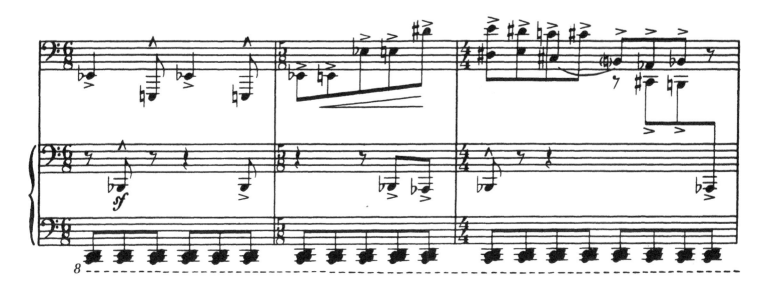

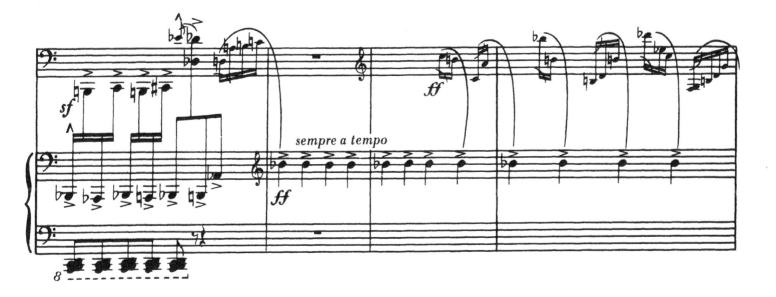

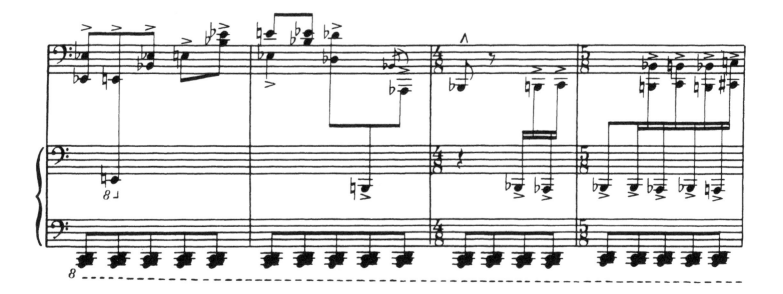

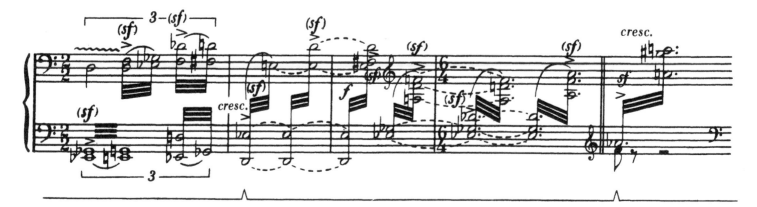

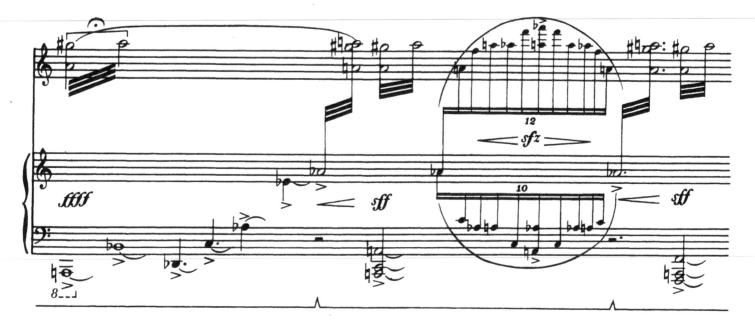

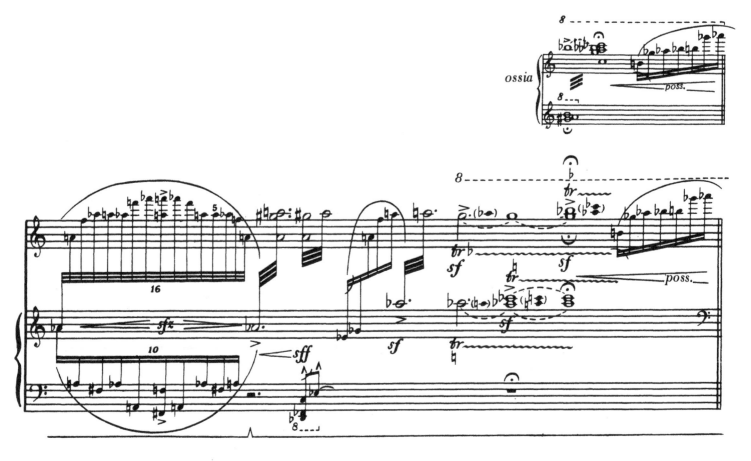

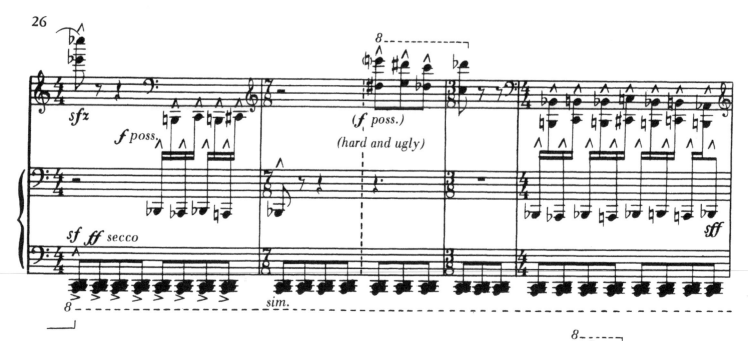

Etude № 5: Melody

*) $\frown$ $\diagdown$ until Db is **pp**

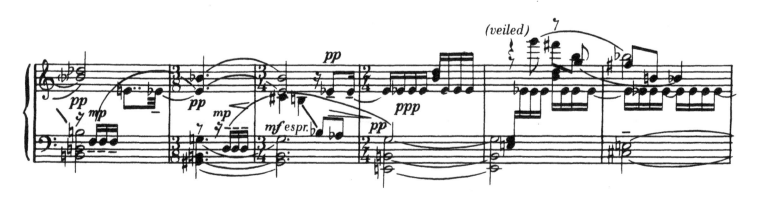

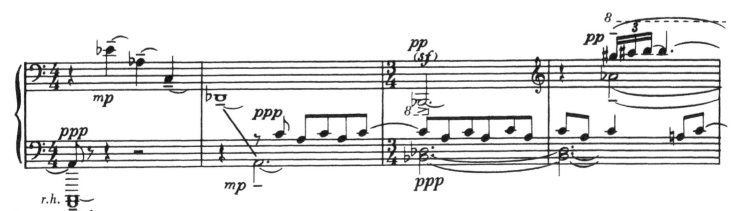